W9-ATA-202

The Presidents of the United States

The Marshall Cavendish illustrated history of

The Presidents of the United States

SEAL OF THE PRESIDENT OF THE UNITED STATES

E PLURIBUS UNUM

Written by
Ruth Oakley

Illustrated by
Steve Lucas and Tim Woodcock-Jones

MARSHALL CAVENDISH
New York · London · Toronto · Sydney

Library Edition Published 1990

Published by Marshall Cavendish Corporation
147, West Merrick Road
Freeport
Long Island
N.Y. 11520

Series created by Graham Beehag Book Design
Designed by Graham Beehag
Produced by DPM Services Limited

Library of Congress Cataloging-in-Publication Data

Oakley, Ruth.
The Marshall Cavendish illustrated history of presidents of the United States / by Ruth Oakley
p. cm.
Includes indexes.
Summary: Places each American preesident in a historical context and discusses his life, with an emphasis on his political activity and presidential term.
ISBN 1-85435-144-3 (set)
1. Presidents – United States – Biography – Juvenile literature. 2. United States – Politics and government – Juvenile literature.
[1. Presidents.] I. Title.
E176.8.025 1990
973'.0992 – dc20 89-17283
[B] CIP
[920] AC

Printed and bound in the United States of America by Lake Book Manufacturing Inc.

CONTENTS

Introduction

With the birth of the twentieth century, the United States began to take its place as one of the major world powers. The transition from a British colony, its economy based on agriculture, to a powerful and wealthy industrial nation drawing its strength from the diverse talents of immigrants from a wide variety of cultures was made plain. By 1913, the U.S. had overtaken Britain to become the world's largest manufacturing nation. This resulted in a concentration of money and power among a few financiers and industrialists. Each of the Presidents from Benjamin Harrison to Woodrow Wilson sought to curb their influence.

A sharp increase in trade led to more concern with

foreign affairs. The U.S. was also directly affected by events taking place in other countries. The Panama Canal was built. In foreign policy, the U.S. was actively involved in Central and South American, Caribbean, Asian, and European affairs during this period. Her entry into World War I had a decisive effect on its outcome and on the efforts of European powers to colonize the rest of the world.

Efforts to reform the political system continued, and there was progress toward social improvements for workers and children. Women gained improved recognition of their rights and were given the vote in the Nineteenth Amendment of 1920. There was little progress, however, toward civil rights for minority races.

The building of the Panama Canal was advantageous to the U.S. and for world trade.

BENJAMIN HARRISON

(1833-1901)

Twenty-third President: 1889-1893

A famous family

Benjamin Harrison was the great-grandson of his namesake Benjamin Harrison, one of the signatories of the Declaration of Independence in 1776, and grandson of William H. "Old Tip" Harrison, who was, briefly, the ninth president of the United States in 1841. Young Benjamin was born on his grandfather's farm in North Bend, Ohio, on August 20, 1833. He was the second child of John Scott Harrison, a farmer, and his second wife, Elizabeth Ramsey Irwin Harrison, who eventually had seven sons and three daughters. Benjamin graduated from Miami University, Oxford, Ohio, with a B.A. in 1852. He studied law and was called to the bar. In 1853, he married Caroline Lavinia Scott, the daughter of a Presbyterian minister and college professor. The couple moved to Indianapolis hoping that life in the West would increase their opportunities. They had a son and a daughter. After Caroline's death in 1892, Benjamin married her niece, Mary Scott Lord Dimmock, who bore him a daughter.

Harrison was elected Indianapolis City Attorney in 1857. During the Civil War, he enlisted as a Union colonel in the Indiana Volunteer Infantry. He fought in Sherman's Atlanta campaign and was promoted to the

Many families moved out West to make new lives for themselves.

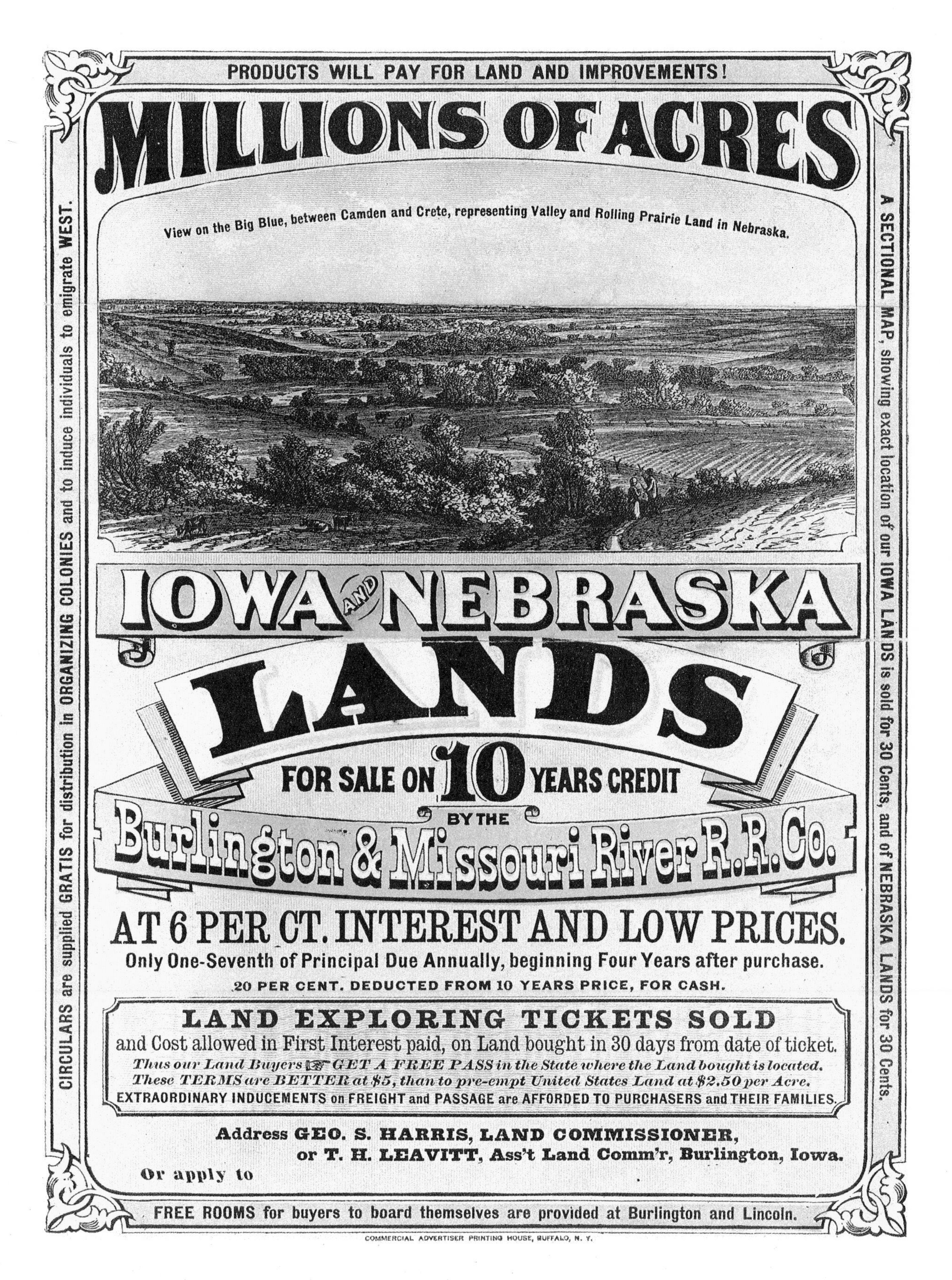
PRODUCTS WILL PAY FOR LAND AND IMPROVEMENTS!
MILLIONS OF ACRES
View on the Big Blue, between Camden and Crete, representing Valley and Rolling Prairie Land in Nebraska.
IOWA AND NEBRASKA
LANDS
FOR SALE ON 10 YEARS CREDIT
BY THE
Burlington & Missouri River R. R. Co.
AT 6 PER CT. INTEREST AND LOW PRICES.
Only One-Seventh of Principal Due Annually, beginning Four Years after purchase.
20 PER CENT. DEDUCTED FROM 10 YEARS PRICE, FOR CASH.
LAND EXPLORING TICKETS SOLD
and Cost allowed in First Interest paid, on Land bought in 30 days from date of ticket.
Thus our Land Buyers ☞ GET A FREE PASS in the State where the Land bought is located.
These TERMS are BETTER at $5, than to pre-empt United States Land at $2.50 per Acre.
EXTRAORDINARY INDUCEMENTS on FREIGHT and PASSAGE are AFFORDED TO PURCHASERS and THEIR FAMILIES.
Address GEO. S. HARRIS, LAND COMMISSIONER,
or T. H. LEAVITT, Ass't Land Comm'r, Burlington, Iowa.
Or apply to
FREE ROOMS for buyers to board themselves are provided at Burlington and Lincoln.
CIRCULARS are supplied GRATIS for distribution in ORGANIZING COLONIES and to induce individuals to emigrate WEST.
A SECTIONAL MAP, showing exact location of our IOWA LANDS is sold for 30 Cents, and of NEBRASKA LANDS for 30 Cents.
COMMERCIAL ADVERTISER PRINTING HOUSE, BUFFALO, N. Y.

There were also opportunities for land speculators to make their fortunes.

rank of brigadier general in recognition of his leadership qualities.

Republican Party power

Harrison was the Republican party candidate for governor of Indiana in 1876. He failed to be elected, but served in the U.S. Senate for a six-year term beginning in 1881. His political career was unspectacular, yet he was chosen as the Republican candidate for the Presidential election of 1888.

He emerged on the eighth ballot as someone with a good war record and a well-respected family name, came from the electorally important state of Ohio, and was not associated with any scandal or corruption. He

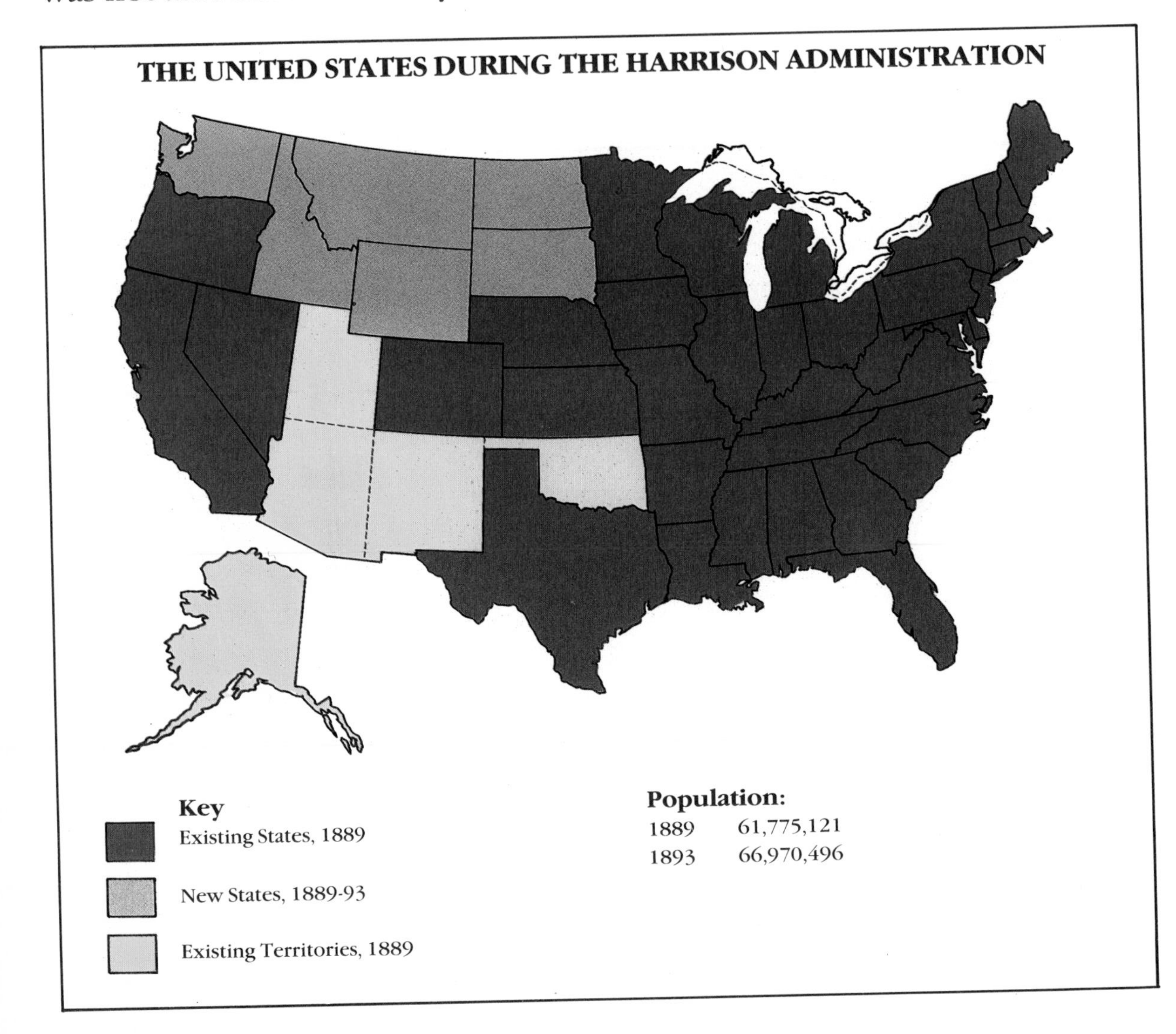

defeated Grover Cleveland, although Cleveland's share of the popular vote exceeded his own. The Republicans won New York State, which was decisive in his victory.

Harrison's Presidency

During his presidency, the Republican party became very powerful; and Harrison himself, although he was honest and conscientious, was not a strong leader. In his campaign, he promised pensions to Civil War veterans. The Disability Pension Act provided pensions no matter how the disabilities were caused, which greatly increased their cost to the government. Large sums were also spent on river and harbor projects and on increasing the navy during his administration.

The struggle between the spoils system and the reform of the Civil Service continued. The Sherman Antitrust Act was an attempt to limit the growing power of industrialists such as John D. Rockefeller in the oil business and Andrew Carnegie in steel.

To please manufacturers, the tariff was increased to a very high rate, 48 percent by the McKinley Tariff Act. The Sherman Silver Purchase Act, which was passed to appease opposition from farmers to the high tariff, led to inflation by increasing the quantities of silver in circulation.

Later life

Harrison did not enjoy his term of office. When he was

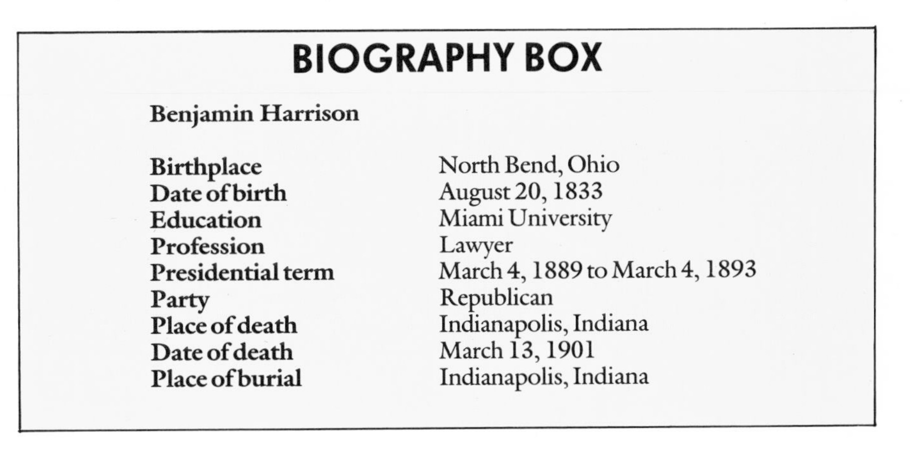

BIOGRAPHY BOX

Benjamin Harrison

Birthplace	North Bend, Ohio
Date of birth	August 20, 1833
Education	Miami University
Profession	Lawyer
Presidential term	March 4, 1889 to March 4, 1893
Party	Republican
Place of death	Indianapolis, Indiana
Date of death	March 13, 1901
Place of burial	Indianapolis, Indiana

defeated in 1892, he was glad to leave the White House and return to his law practice. In 1899, he represented Venezuela in negotiations in Paris over a boundary dispute with Britain.

He died in Indianapolis in 1901 and is buried there.

Thomas Edison was one of several great American inventors of the late nineteenth and early twentieth centuries.

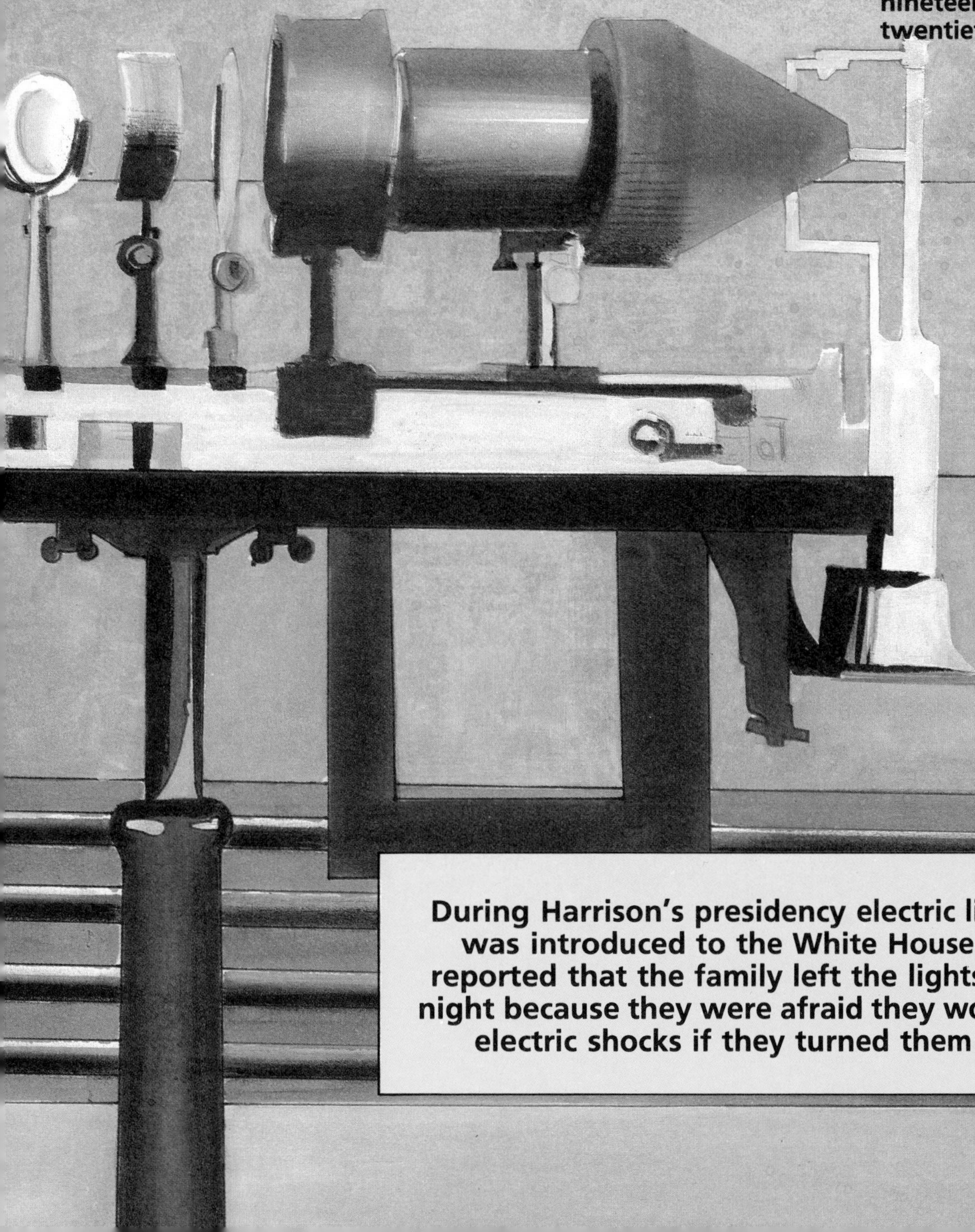

During Harrison's presidency electric lighting was introduced to the White House. It is reported that the family left the lights on all night because they were afraid they would get electric shocks if they turned them off.

WILLIAM McKINLEY

(1843-1901)

Twenty-fifth President: 1897-1901

(For Twenty-fourth President, Grover Cleveland, see Vol. 4 page 54)

Family and early life

William McKinley was born in Niles, Trumbull County, Ohio, on January 29, 1843, the seventh child of nine born to William McKinley, an iron founder, and his wife, Nancy Campbell Allison McKinley. The family moved to Poland, Ohio, to give the children better educational opportunities, but William's education at Allegheny College, Meadville, Pennsylvania, was cut short because of illness and lack of money. He began work as a teacher and post office clerk. When Fort Sumter was attacked, McKinley enlisted and fought bravely on the Union side during the Civil War. He was promoted to the rank of brevet major in recognition of his courage and leadership.

After the war, McKinley studied law and graduated from Albany Law School, New York. He opened a practice in Canton, Ohio, where he was elected District Attorney from 1869 to 1871. It was here that he met Ida Saxton, who was working as a cashier in her father's bank. She was well-educated, pretty, and fashionable.

They married in 1871, and their first daughter, Katherine, was born on Christmas Day that year. When their second child, another daughter, was born

McKinley was the last Civil War veteran to become President. He had fought under Rutherford Hayes. He was also the first president from an industrial family.

in April, 1873, Ida was very ill. The baby was weak and only lived for four months.

Ida never recovered, and the McKinleys' sorrows intensified when Katherine also died in 1876. Ida suffered from epilepsy and was generally weak and in poor health, but she took her place by McKinley's side as hostess in the White House although she was an invalid. When she was about to have a seizure, William would place a large handkerchief over her face.

McKinley delivers the inaugural address.

McKinley's political career

McKinley was elected to the House of Representatives as a Republican in 1877 and served there for fourteen years. He was a member of the Ways and Means Committee and became its Chairman in 1889. The McKinley Tariff Act of 1890, which set the tariff at the high rate of forty-eight percent, made his name well-known. He was Governor of Ohio from 1892 to 1896, which gave him a great deal of administrative experience that was very useful when he became President.

In 1896, with the support of Marcus A. Hanna, a wealthy and powerful Ohio businessman, he was elected on the first ballot as the presidential candidate for the Republican party. After a fiercely fought campaign, he defeated William Jennings Bryan in the election for the Presidency.

The blowing up of the U.S.S. *Maine* in Havana harbor in 1898 precipitated the Spanish-American war.

His Presidency

Gold was discovered in Alaska, Colorado, and South Africa, and the economic depression in America, which had dominated the election campaign, was coming to an end. The Gold Standard Act of 1900 made gold the standard on which the stability of the U.S. currency depended. Cuba was in revolt from Spain. There was a great deal of American investment in the island, and many newspapers and politicians in the U.S. were calling for the country to go to war with Spain. McKinley wanted peace, but after the U.S.S. *Maine* was destroyed in Havana Harbor, he allowed Congress to declare war in April, 1898.

Spain was defeated, and the war was ended by the Treaty of Paris in 1898. Cuba became independent, and the U.S. gained Puerto Rico, Guam and the Philippines. Hawaii was annexed during the course of

The U.S. press held Spain responsible for the deaths of two hundred and sixty U.S. sailors aboard the *Maine*.

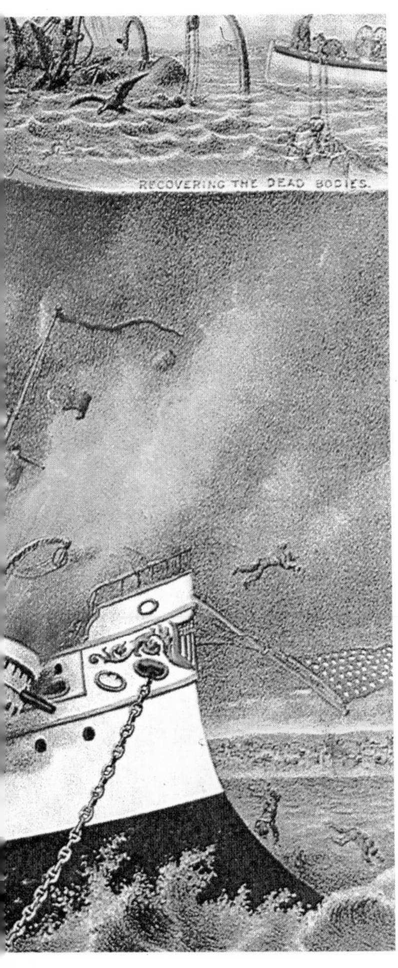

McKinley's assassination stunned the nation.

BIOGRAPHY BOX

William McKinley

Birthplace	Niles, Ohio
Date of birth	January 29, 1843
Education	Allegheny College and Albany Law School
Profession	Lawyer
Presidential term	March 4, 1897 to September 14, 1901
Party	Republican
Place of death	Buffalo, New York
Date of death	September 14, 1901
Place of death	Canton, Ohio

THE UNITED STATES DURING THE McKINLEY ADMINISTRATION

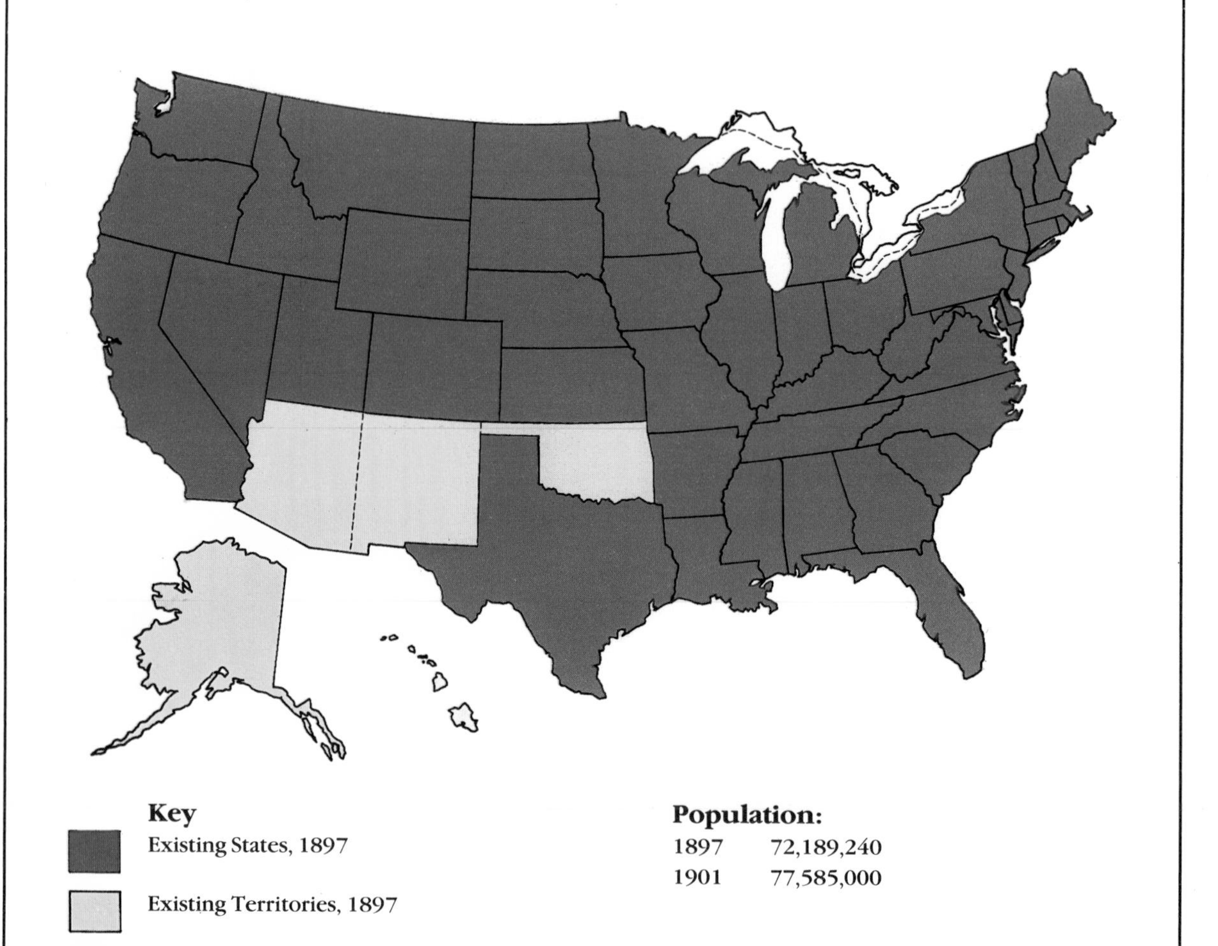

The Klondike Gold Rush of 1897 helped to improve the economic situation.

Pearl King of the Pacific.

SUNDAY EXAMINER.

The Examiner.

Most Picturesque of Pirates

SUNDAY EXAMINER.

VOL. XLV. SAN FRANCISCO, MONDAY MORNING, AUGUST 30, 1897. NO. 61.

LITTLE GOLD AND HARD-LUCK STORIES ON THE PORTLAND.

She Brought Out Less Than $100,000.

This Was Divided Among a Lucky Thirteen.

Last Man From Klondyke Tells Discouraging Tales.

Four Men Lost by the Capsizing of a Fishing Boat.

By Arthur H. Barendt.

Tim Bell	$30,000
C. K. Zilly	5,000
W. Zahn	2,000
G. S. Lansing	2,000
A. Buckling	1,800
. Rowan	5,000
Wm Oler	3,000
Joe Goldsmith	15,000
N. W. Powers	5,000
W. W. Caldwell	4,000
M. R. Gowler	5,000
F. W. Cobb	3,000
B. Fermins	2,000

Death for Two Who Made Fortunes.

Privations of Many in Search of Gold.

Beaching of the River Steamer Hamilton on the Yukon.

Soft-Muscled Clerks Soon Tired of a Hard Life.

By Edward H. Hamilton.

SCENES ALONG THE NEW WHITE PASS ROUTE TO THE GOLD FIELDS NEAR DAWSON.

These are the first authentic pictures ever published of the new trail from Skaguay to the Klondyke. Reproduced from photographs taken expressly for "The Examiner" by a member of one of the first expeditions to reach the new El Dorado via the White Pass.

BEAR FROM THE YUKON.

Petersen Tells of Those Who Did Not Succeed.

An Accident Near Skaguay Which Resulted in the Loss of Four Lives.

Continued on Page Five.

the war. The United States was emerging as a world power.

McKinley was elected for a second term in 1900, with Theodore Roosevelt as Vice-President. He was by now extremely popular, and on September 6, 1901, he went to a large reception held in his honor at the Pan-American Exposition in Buffalo. There, a Czech anarchist, Leon Czolgosz, shot him twice at close range. The President died eight days later with Ida by his side.

THEODORE ROOSEVELT

(1858-1919)

Twenty-sixth President: 1901-1909

Theodore Roosevelt

Family background

In some ways, Theodore Roosevelt was more like the early presidents than his immediate predecessors in the office. He was born in 1858 into an old and rich family in New York City. His father, also called Theodore, was a merchant banker of Dutch descent and Collector of the Port of New York.

The young Theodore did not have to struggle to make his way in the world. He began with many social and educational advantages. Because of his poor health, including asthma and poor eyesight, he was taught at home by private tutors instead of going to school. In an effort to improve his health, he was taken on trips to Europe, which broadened his experience.

As he grew up, he exercised and built up his stamina. His health improved enough for him to be admitted to Harvard College, where he excelled at sports. He graduated with a B.A. and unlike most politicians of his time, was a scholar who wrote books on topics unrelated to politics. The other side of his character was the man of action, who enjoyed hunting and an adventurous life.

In 1880, his graduation year, Roosevelt married Alice Hathaway Lee. She died in 1884, leaving a two-day-old daughter named after her. Roosevelt's mother

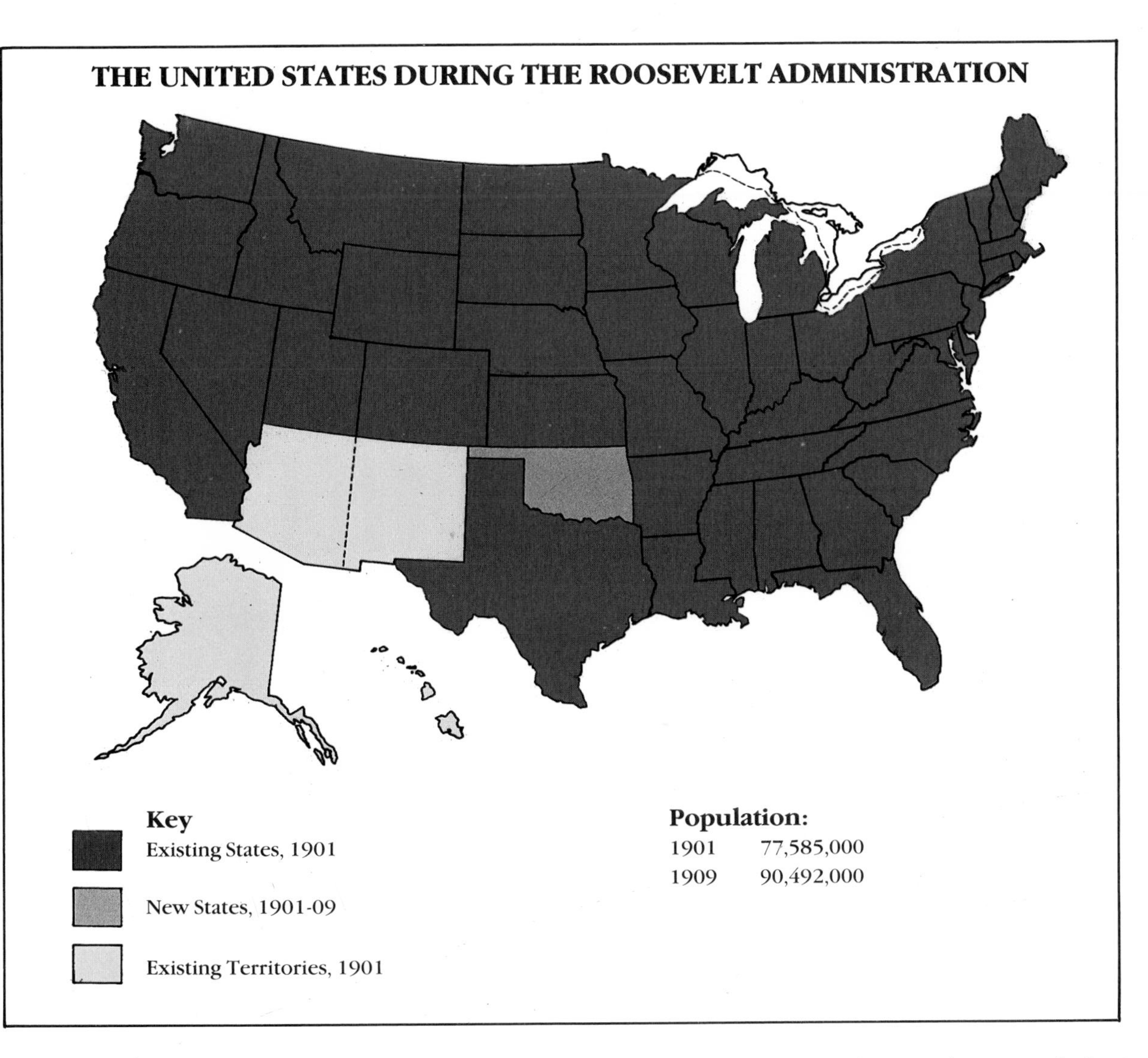

died the day after his wife. During this sad period, he withdrew from political life and tried to ease his sorrow with a period of strenuous physical activity in the West.

Two years later in London, Theodore remarried a childhood friend, Edith Kermit Carow. They had five more children, four sons and another daughter. Edith was a loving and capable wife and mother, who shared Theodore's love of literature and his scholarly interests. During his presidency, the White House was refurbished and became the center of the country's social life. Their private home was Sagamore Hill in Oyster Bay, Long Island, where Edith continued to live after Theodore died, until her own death in 1945.

Roosevelt's Rough Riders storm San Juan Hill in the war against Spain in Cuba.

Roosevelt's early career

Roosevelt began his political career at a young age, entering the New York State Legislature in Albany as a Republican when he was only twenty-three. His first wife's death coincided with an unsuccessful bid for the Republican Presidential candidacy, and Roosevelt withdrew from political life.

He went to Dakota Territory, where he bought and ran two ranches. He was elected Deputy Sheriff of Billings County. At the same time, he also tried to write books.

After his second marriage and his return to the east, Roosevelt tried to re-enter politics. He ran for Mayor of New York, but failed to be elected. He then wrote many books, including "The Winning of the West." In 1889 he was appointed as a Civil Service Commissioner by President Benjamin Harrison. In

1895, he was appointed president of the Board of Police Commissioners for New York City during Grover Cleveland's second term as President. In both of these jobs, Roosevelt displayed great energy and vigor. His efforts at reform made him enemies among those who were benefiting from the spoils system and the power of the political parties.

Roosevelt was Assistant Secretary of the Navy when the war with Spain over Cuba was brewing. In 1898, he resigned to fight. As Lt. Colonel of the First Volunteer Cavalry Regiment, or the "Rough Riders," he became famous when he led them in the storming of San Juan Hill in Cuba.

On his return to New York, Roosevelt ran for governor of New York state. His candidacy was

Roosevelt and the Rough Riders pose for a photograph at the top of San Juan Hill.

A cartoonist's version of Roosevelt's arrival in San Antonio for a Rough Riders reunion.

candidacy was supported by the Republican party "boss," Tom Platt, who wanted to distract attention from party corruption and scandal in the state.

After his election, Roosevelt was a more energetic and reforming Governor than Platt had bargained for. For this reason, Platt made sure that Roosevelt was nominated as vice-presidential candidate in the 1900 election. He felt that it was unlikely that Roosevelt

Edith Roosevelt decided that portraits of all the First Ladies should be hung in the ground floor corridors of the White House. During Roosevelt's administration the President's residence in Washington was given its official designation as the White House.

would have any real power as Vice-President. The assassin, Leon Czolgosz, guaranteed that this was not to be the case when he shot President McKinley in Buffalo on September 6, 1901. Roosevelt was recalled from a hunting trip in the Adirondacks Mountains to take the oath of office and became President on September 14, 1901.

Roosevelt's first Presidency and the square deal

Roosevelt took office at the beginning of a new century and presided over a period of great change in American life. The U.S. was becoming a world power and a great and wealthy manufacturing nation. Although he came from a privileged background, Roosevelt was well aware of how unevenly America's wealth was distributed, and he cared about social injustice.

A few powerful industrialists and financiers, men such as Edward H. Harrigan, Andrew Carnegie, John D. Rockefeller, and John Pierpoint Morgan, wielded enormous power and took little interest in the sufferings of the workers who labored to produce the wealth. Wages were low, safety regulations virtually non-existent, and child labor was common.

Many groups were campaigning for social reform. Roosevelt was more conservative in his ideas than they were, and more aware of the dangers of the power of the mob, but he recognized that changes were needed and gave publicity to the reformers' demands. His "Square Deal" was an attempt to give workers some rights and to provide them with a reasonable standard of living without destroying the profitability and progress of the big business on which the nation's prosperity depended.

He attempted to limit the power of wealthy financiers and industrialists such as Morgan and Rockefeller by invoking the Sherman Antitrust Act of 1890 and by dissolving the Northern Securities Company in 1904. This action prevented Harriman from achieving his aim of monopoly control of all the railroad companies across the country.

Miners, led by John Mitchell of the United Mine Workers Union, went on strike in 1902 in protest against their appalling working and living conditions. The operators, appointed by Morgan, refused to recognize the Union or to negotiate until the men returned to work; the workers refused to return to the

Theodore Roosevelt as the Apostle of Prosperity on a Republican poster.

Children worked long hours in dangerous conditions such as in this glass factory.

mines until their bosses improved conditions and pay. The nation was beginning to run out of coal, and winter was approaching. Roosevelt intervened and insisted that an arbitration commission should be set up. As a result, the workers were given a ten percent pay increase, and anthracite supplies were resumed.

In 1903, the President set up the Bureau of Corporations to research the dealings of big business and make their findings public.

The second term

Roosevelt succeeded in negotiating the right to build the Panama Canal.

Roosevelt's social reforms were popular with the general public, and he was re-elected with a large majority in 1904. One of his great interests was nature, and he took an active interest in the conservation of natural resources like forests, minerals, and water supplies. In 1906, Roosevelt established Yosemite National Park and set aside forest lands, coal deposits, and sites for future dams which were not to be encroached upon by railroads or other big businesses. In 1907, the Inland Waterways Commission was set up. A National Conservation Conference was held in the White House the following year.

A book called "The Jungle," which exposed the exploitation of labor and the poor hygiene in the Chicago stockyards, gave rise to the Meat Inspection Act and the Pure Food and Drugs Act of 1906. Both gave some limited protection to the consumer for the first time. The Hepburn Act, which regulated the charges which railroads could make, extended consumer protection further.

Foreign policy and the Panama Canal

The United States continued to expand its influence abroad, especially in China and in Central and South America. In return for Roosevelt's recognition in 1903 of the new Republic in Panama, formerly a province of Colombia, the Americans were allowed to buy the Canal Zone for $10,000,000 and to build the Panama Canal.

The educationalist, Booker T. Washington, who built Tuskegee Institute in Alabama into a college, was the first black person to be officially entertained in the White House. When he dined with Theodore Roosevelt in 1901, there was strong criticism from the southern press.

Despite illness in his youth Roosevelt worked to build up his fitness. He loved the outdoor life and the danger and excitement of hunting.

American naval forces and merchant ships were then able to sail from the Atlantic to the Pacific Ocean without having to go right around South America and Cape Horn. Now that the United States had possessions in the Caribbean and the Pacific, naval access was more important, and the shortened voyages saved time and money.

The Roosevelt Corollary to the Monroe Doctrine asserted that, if any country in the western hemisphere failed to govern itself adequately, the United States must act as a policing power to enforce civilized standards. Roosevelt formulated the doctrine to justify his supervision of Santo Domingo's finances when the republic failed to pay its foreign debts.

In 1906, Roosevelt was awarded the Nobel Peace Prize for his initiatives a year earlier to end the Russo-Japanese War with the Treaty of Portsmouth. He supported the idea of international arbitration when he sent a dispute with Mexico to the International Court at the Hague. At another Hague peace conference in 1907, attended by forty-four countries, Roosevelt instructed the American delegation to negotiate a cessation of the competition between countries in building up arms.

After the Presidency

Roosevelt did not stand for a third term, in accordance with the precedent set by George Washington. He did, however, make sure that his choice of candidate, William H. Taft, was adopted by the Republicans. Roosevelt first turned to writing to supplement his income and then went to Africa to hunt big game.

After a tour of Europe, he returned to the U.S. Because he was disappointed with Taft's performance as President, considering his policies to be too conservative, Roosevelt agreed to run for a third term as President in the 1912 election. He was the Progressive candidate, while Taft remained the official Republican candidate and Woodrow Wilson ran for the Democrats. The result of splitting the Republican vote between Roosevelt and Taft was that Wilson won the election.

In 1914, Roosevelt undertook his last adventure — an exploration into the wilds of Brazil. He opposed Wilson's policy of American neutrality in World War I, holding the view that America should support the Allies. He was also against the League of Nations, which was formed after the war.

He died in his sleep at home on January 6, 1919.

BIOGRAPHY BOX

Theodore Roosevelt

Birthplace	New York, New York
Date of birth	October 27, 1858
Education	Harvard
Profession	Lawyer
Presidential term	September 14, 1901 to March 4, 1909
Party	Republican
Place of death	Oyster Bay, New York
Date of death	January 6, 1919
Place of burial	Oyster Bay, New York

WILLIAM H. TAFT

(1857-1930)

Twenty-seventh President: 1909-1913

William Taft came to the Presidency at the age of fifty-one with considerable experience of public life. He had served the nation in several offices of state, and he was the man Theodore Roosevelt wished to succeed him, an influential aspect of Taft's election.

Taft was, however, a very different personality from his predecessor. He was not a politician by profession, but a lawyer. He believed that the president of the United States should act only when specifically empowered to do so by the Constitution. Roosevelt, on the other hand, felt free to make decisions except when forbidden by law to do so. Taft was cautious and conservative in attitude. Eventually, this fundamental difference of approach caused a rift between them, and Roosevelt ran against Taft in the 1912 election.

Childhood, family, and marriage

William Howard Taft was born on September 15, 1857, at 2038 Auburn Avenue, Cincinnati, Ohio. He was the second child of Alphonso Taft, a lawyer and politician (who had been an ambassador to Austria and Russia under Chester C. Arthur) and his second wife, Louisa Maria Torrey Taft. Eventually, there were five children of this second marriage, and Taft had two

Taft had Roosevelt's support on the campaign trail.

Taft was the heaviest man to be President; he weighed three hundred and fifty pounds. It was said that that he once gave up his seat on a street car to three ladies. A special bathtub was installed for him in the White House.

half-brothers from his father's first marriage.

Taft graduated from Yale College with a B.A. in 1878. He continued his studies at Cincinnati Law School, where he received his L.L.B. in 1880.

In 1879, he met Helen "Nellie" Herron, the daughter of Harriet Collins and John Herron, a Cincinnati lawyer and one of the city's leading Republicans. Over a period of years, the couple's friendship and shared interests grew into love, and they were married in 1886.

They had two sons and a daughter. When Taft lived abroad and traveled in the course of his career, Nellie and the children went with him. During their period at the White House, they hosted many glittering social occasions. Among the family celebrations held in the White House were the debut of their daughter, Helen, during the Christmas season of 1910 and their Silver Wedding Anniversary garden party on June 19, 1911.

Lawyer and Governor

Taft was a judge in the Ohio Superior Court from 1887-1900. He was U.S. Solicitor General from 1890-2 and a U.S. circuit court judge from 1892-1900. In 1900, Roosevelt sent him as President of the Philippines Commission to deal with a rebellion of the islands' inhabitants against America's annexation after

Helen Taft arranged for three thousand Japanese cherry trees to be planted around the Tidal Basin in Washington. They still serve as a memorial to her when they bloom each spring.

Election material produced by the Republican Party for the successful 1908 campaign.

the Spanish-American War. He became Governor General of the Philippines in the following year and remained in the position until 1904. He carried out a thorough reorganization of the country, improving its roads, education, sanitation, health, and economy, and was popular with the Filipinos, whom he treated as equals.

He then became Secretary of War until 1908. In this capacity, he oversaw the building of the Panama Canal. In 1906, at Cuba's request for U.S. assistance, Taft was sent to take charge of the island and restore its peace and stability.

Taft's Presidency

In the 1908 election, Taft decisively beat the Democrat candidate William Jenning Bryan, who was making his third try for the presidency. During his campaign, Taft had pledged to revise the tariff. The general assumption was that the revision would be downward, but the Senate revised the bill which had been passed by the House of Representatives and put up the rates on many items. Enraged Progressive Republicans fought the proposals, but Taft eventually signed the bill.

Taft continued Roosevelt's antitrust policy, notably with the Mann-Elkins Act, which brought railroad rates under government control. During his administration, parcel post and postal savings banks were introduced. Legislation was passed to regulate and improve working and safety conditions in mines and on railroads. The Children's Bureau was established to monitor child labor at a national level. The Sixteenth Amendment, endorsed by Taft in 1913, authorized a federal income tax. The dismissal of Gifford Pinchot, the Chief Forester appointed by

BIOGRAPHY BOX

William Howard Taft

Birthplace	Cincinnati, Ohio
Date of birth	September 15, 1857
Education	Yale
Profession	Lawyer
Presidential term	March 4, 1909 to March 4, 1913
Party	Republican
Place of death	Washington, D.C.
Date of death	March 8, 1930
Place of burial	Arlington National Cemetery,

Civil War broke out in Mexico, but Taft sent U.S. troops no further than the border.

Roosevelt, was a further cause of dissension between Taft and Roosevelt. Taft was defeated by Woodrow Wilson in the 1912 election; the intervention of Roosevelt as a Progressive candidate split the Republican vote.

Later life

Taft was appointed as professor of constitutional law at Yale University in 1913. In 1921, President Harding appointed him to the post of Chief Justice of the United States, which had been Taft's dearest ambition. He retired in February, 1930, and died a month later. He is buried at Arlington National Cemetery, Virginia.

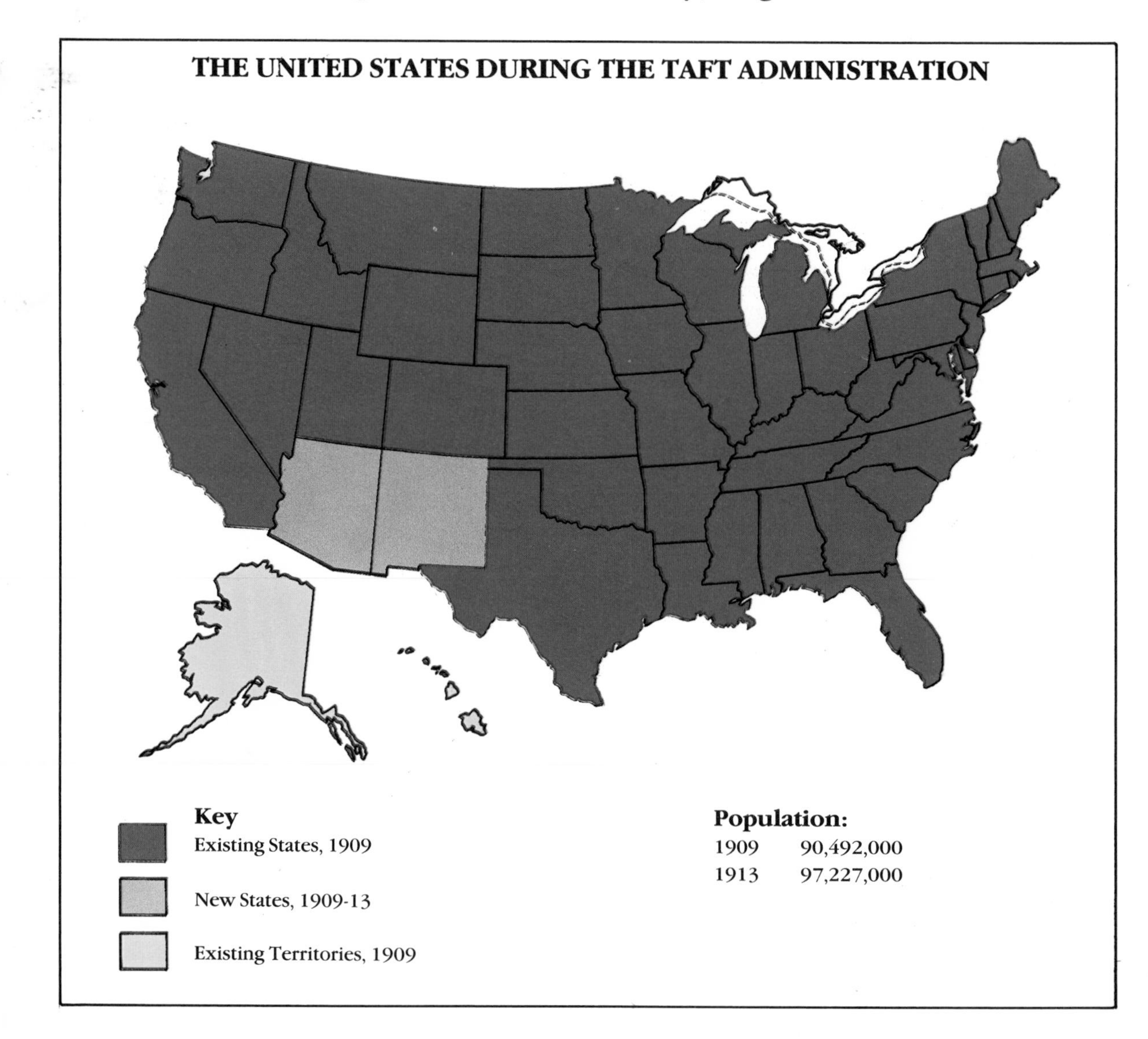

WOODROW WILSON

(1856-1924)

Twenty-eighth President: 1913-1921

Early life

Thomas Woodrow Wilson was born in a manse at 24 North Coalter Street, Staunton, Virginia, on December 28, 1856. His father was Joseph Ruggles Wilson, a Presbyterian minister. His mother, Jessie Woodrow, was born in Carlisle, England, the daughter of a Presbyterian minister. Woodrow was the third of their four children. The family moved many times. During the Civil War, Reverend Wilson supported the Confederacy. His church became a hospital, and Yankee prisoners of war were kept in a stockade in the churchyard.

Education

When he was seventeen, Woodrow went to a Presbyterian college in North Carolina, where he showed an aptitude for debating. He continued his education by entering Princeton College in the New Jersey countryside in September, 1875. Princeton was then a private college without the distinguished reputation it earned later. Wilson's academic leanings were toward politics and history, and he continued his interest in debating. At this time, he formed his intention to enter political life.

After graduating from Princeton with a B.A. in 1879,

Although he was a serious scholar and a religious man who read the Bible every day, Woodrow Wilson had a lighter side to his nature. He was a good tap dancer and entertained his family by reciting limericks and doing impersonations, including one of Theodore Roosevelt.

he returned to Virginia to study law at the state university. He continued his interest in debating and in reading history, political science, and literature, but he was "most terribly bored by the noble study of the Law." He became ill and returned to his parents' home at Wilmington to continue his studies. He tried unsuccessfully to set up a law practice in Atlanta with a friend from the university.

Marriage and academic career

In 1883, while on a visit to Rome, Georgia, Wilson again met Ellen Louise Axson, whose father was also a Presbyterian minister. They had first met when Woodrow was six and Ellen a baby. Ellen was keeping house for her father after her mother's death, and her devotion to her father delayed her marriage to Woodrow until 1885.

Meanwhile, Woodrow enrolled in the graduate school of Johns Hopkins University in Baltimore. In 1884, he published "Congressional Government," a book about American government, which was well received and enhanced his reputation as a scholar. Wilson received his doctorate from Johns Hopkins in 1886.

Wilson did nothing to support the cause of votes for women until the contribution of women to the war effort brought about a change in public opinion.

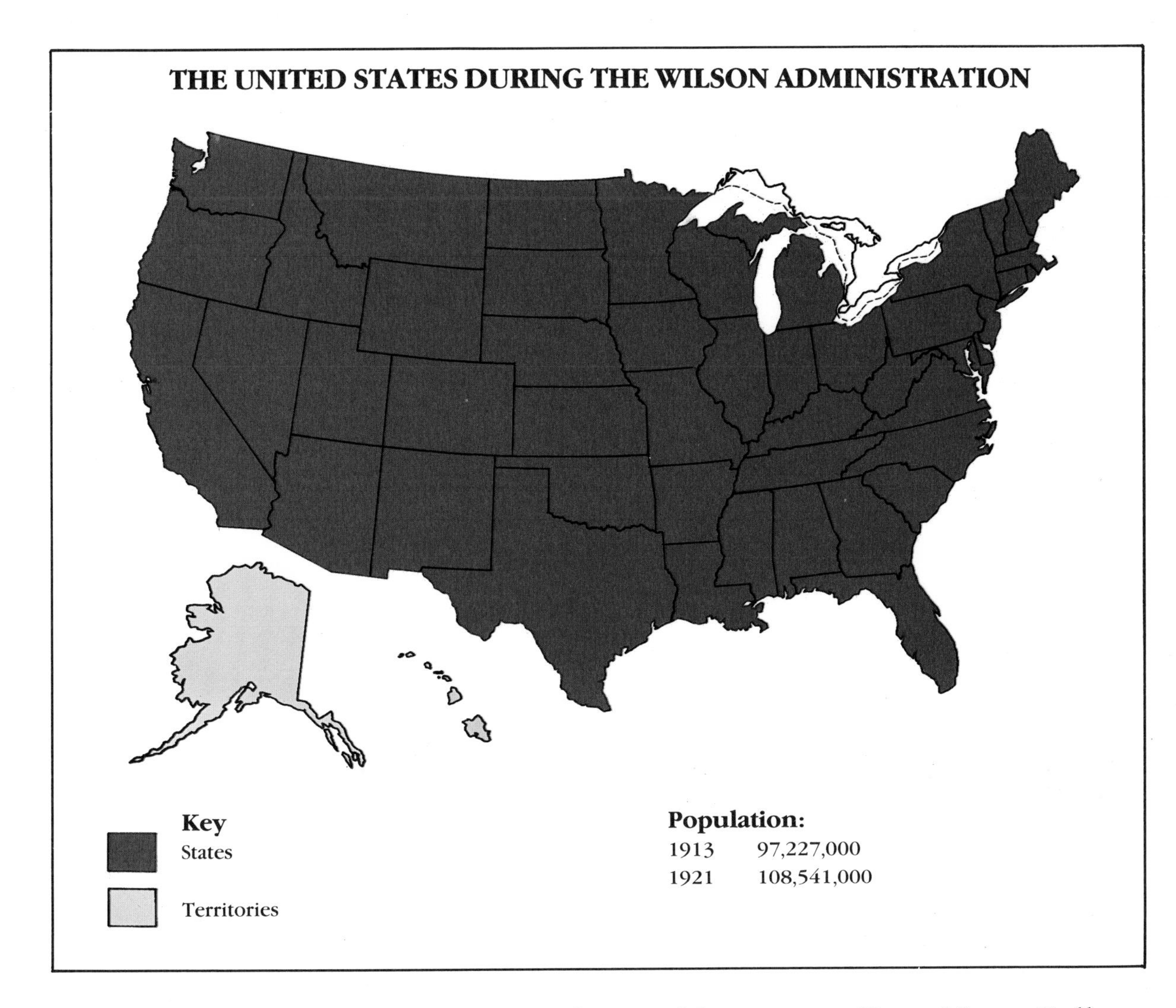

He accepted a teaching post at Bryn Mawr College, Pennsylvania, in 1885, although he still nursed the ambition to enter active politics. He and Ellen lived near the campus with Ellen's young brother. They had three daughters: Margaret, Jessie and Eleanor.

Wilson moved to the Wesleyan University, Connecticut, before accepting a position as Professor of Jurisprudence and Political Economy at his old college, Princeton, in 1890. He became its President in 1902 after turning down several offers from other universities.

He reformed the system of teaching in the university and made it one of the foremost in the U.S., basing his ideas on what he had seen at Oxford University in England on two brief trips there. His efforts impaired his health and made him enemies in the college.

General John J. Pershing, Commander of the American Expedition Force in Europe formed the 1st U.S. Army in July 1918. This was the first U.S. Army to see action in Europe.

Political career

So, Wilson was looking for a change and readily accepted the offer of George M. Harvey, an influential newspaperman, to promote him as the Democratic candidate for the governor of New Jersey. With the support of Senator James Smith, New Jersey's Democratic boss, Wilson was elected by a majority of almost 50,000 votes in 1910.

As governor, Wilson introduced popular measures to prevent corruption in politics and business. Other laws gave ordinary voters the power to select candidates by means of primary elections.

Wilson's Presidency

His successful governorship, allied to his considerable academic reputation, made Wilson a strong Democratic presidential candidate in the 1912 election. The Republicans' chances were weakened by having Taft as their official candidate while Roosevelt ran as a Progressive. Wilson campaigned for the rights of the individual against the power of the privileged and wealthy few. He was elected with a record majority of electoral votes.

One of his first actions was to bring in a bill to reduce the tariff. The Underwood Tariff Act was passed in 1913 despite strong opposition. The same year, the Federal Reserve Act transferred the responsibility for the supply of money from independent banks to the government by setting up twelve Regional Reserve Banks across the country. In 1914, Wilson continued the antitrust policy of

When the United States entered World War I, there were only 200,000 men in the army. By the end, there were 4,000,000. About 1,004,000 American troops fought in the war.

Roosevelt and Taft with the Clayton Antitrust Act. This law tightened up the Sherman Act of 1890, which lawyers had been able to circumvent on behalf of the powerful bankers and industrialists.

In foreign policy, Wilson strove to keep the U.S. at peace with her Central and South American and Caribbean neighbors. During a period of revolution in Mexico from 1914-7, he authorized the bombardment and occupation of Vera Cruz by American forces in April, 1914. Eventually, peace was brought about with

The sinking of the *Lusitania* by Germany influenced U.S. public opinion toward entering World War I to aid the Allies.

the help of negotiations by Brazil, Chile, and Argentina. Wilson also found it necessary to send U.S. forces to Haiti in 1915 after several revolutionary uprisings there.

Wilson drafted a treaty to heal the breach with Colombia which had been caused by Roosevelt's

LUSITANIA

VOTE FOR
WILSON
AND
MARSHALL
SEABURY
AND
McCOMBS
WOMENS BUREAU
DEMOCRATIC NATIONAL COMMITTEE
FOR
PRESIDENT
WOODROW
WILSON
WHO BROKE TH
MONEY TRUST
WHO KEEPS US
OUT OF WAR?
WHO STANDS FOR
THE 8 HOUR DAY?
WHO EXTENDED
THE PARCEL POST?
WHO GAVE THE FARMER
RURAL CREDITS?

One of Wilson's campaign automobiles showing the key points of his campaign policy.

seizure of Panama in order to build the Panama Canal, now nearing completion. In its final form, as passed by Congress, the treaty authorized the payment of a twenty-five million dollar indemnity to Colombia and allowed her citizens to use the canal on the same terms as those of the U.S.

In 1914, Wilson suffered personal tragedy when Ellen died in August. He grieved bitterly. He was remarried in December, 1915, to Edith Bolling Galt, a widow. Ellen had told her physician the day before she died that she wished him to tell her husband that she hoped he would marry again. Edith and Woodrow were very happy together, and when he suffered a stroke in 1919, she was very supportive.

War in Europe

In 1914, war in Europe erupted. Wilson urged that the U.S. should remain neutral. At first, it was a generally popular view. Many U.S. citizens were German, Austrian or Irish immigrants; and in any case, most Americans at the time did not wish to become involved with a struggle between the European powers. During the course of the war, public and government opinion began to change, partially as a result of a series of attacks by German submarines on merchant ships which caused the loss of American lives. The first incident was the sinking of the British liner, the *Lusitania*. One hundred and twenty-eight Americans were among the twelve hundred civilians who died. Wilson sent a series of Notes to Germany, but still refused to be drawn into the war, realizing all the suffering it would bring to American citizens.

Industrial production was standardized to eliminate waste and increase efficiency as part of the war effort. New regulations to control the manufacture of corsets released eight thousand tons of steel each year to use for munitions.

Woodrow Wilson asks a crowded Senate to declare war on Germany.

Wilson was re-elected in 1916 and continued his efforts at mediation between Britain and the Allies on one side, and Germany and the Central Powers on the other. His suggestion that a league of nations should impose peace was rejected.

America enters the war

The attacks on shipping by German submarines continued. Early in 1917, a telegram from the German Foreign Secretary, Alfred Zimmerman, to the German Minister in Mexico City was intercepted and decoded by British Intelligence. It contained secret proposals for an alliance between Mexico and Germany, which would return Texas, New Mexico, and Arizona to Mexico if she helped Germany win the war.

Wilson felt that under these circumstances the United States had to enter the war on the side of the

Allies. After a long debate, Congress agreed on April 6, 1917. Once America's industrial and military strength was put to the service of the Allied cause, the final defeat of Germany and the Central Powers was never in doubt.

Final disappointment

Wilson felt deeply and passionately that unless lessons were learned and a mechanism for keeping peace between nations was set up, the tragedy and waste of war would be repeated. When he attended the peace conference at Versailles in France, he put forward his "Fourteen Points," which he saw as necessary for future security. Although he did not succeed in getting them all accepted and he was disheartened by the vengeful attitude of the victors, his idea to form a League of Nations was accepted in Europe. It was a bitter disappointment to Wilson that the Republican Senate at home refused to accept the peace treaty. His determination to undertake an exhausting countrywide tour to gain popular support for it led to a stroke.

Millions of Allied soldiers died on the battlefields of France in World War I.

With Edith's help, he struggled on until he was succeeded at the White House by President Harding in 1921. Wilson was awarded the Nobel Peace Prize in December, 1920. Although the stroke did not affect his mental ability, he never recovered physically. His last public performance was a speech from his balcony on Armistice Day in November, 1923. He died at home in his sleep on February 3, 1924.

The League of Nations held out hope for the future in Europe, but the idea was not accepted by the U.S. Senate.

BIOGRAPHY BOX

Thomas Woodrow Wilson

Birthplace	Staunton, Virginia
Date of birth	December 28, 1856
Education	Princeton
Profession	Teacher
Presidential term	March 4, 1913 to March 4, 1921
Party	Democrat
Place of death	Washington, D.C.
Date of death	February 3, 1924
Place of burial	Washington, D.C.

GLOSSARY

admit or call to the bar — be qualified to practice as a lawyer
Allies — Britain, France, Russia, and those European countries which opposed Germany in World War I from 1914 to 1918
anarchist — one who believes that all governments should be abolished
anthracite — good quality, hard coal for household use
arbitration — the settlement of a dispute, usually by individuals who are not involved in the dispute
ballot — taking of a vote, either in secret by marking a piece of paper or by a show of hands at a meeting
B.A. — a Bachelor of Arts degree
bill — a suggested law; when a bill has been passed, it becomes an act
campus — the grounds of a school, college or university
Central Powers — Germany and the Austro-Hungarian Empire before and during World War I
circumvent — go around, avoid
civil service — the non-military branches of the administration of a government. Civil servants are appointed, not elected
conservative — wishing to keep things as they are; not wanting rapid change
constitution — the laws and agreements which give a government its powers
corollary — a further statement added to an original one or coming from it
debut — first formal appearance in "society"
depression — a time when people lose confidence in the business dealings of a country. Trade slumps, causing large losses and great financial hardship

GLOSSARY

doctorate — the highest university degree
federal — relating to the central government of a group of states who have agreed to unite, as distinct from the governments of the individual states
financier — one who makes money by borrowing, lending and selling money
indemnity — compensation paid for a loss
industrialist — one who makes money from manufacturing and trade
insurrection — open resistance to established authority
L.L.B. — a Bachelor of Laws degree
legation — a diplomatic minister and his advisers
monopoly — the sole right or ability to trade in a particular commodity or business
Monroe Doctrine — the policy, formulated by President Monroe, of objecting to and preventing interference by European powers in Latin America
precedent — a previous case which is an example, usually a legal term
primary election — an election to select candidates for a main election
province — territory outside a country, but governed by it
spoils system — the custom of rewarding an official's campaign supporters with government posts and removing those who did not help in the campaign
tariff — a law imposing customs duties on exports and imports. In the United States in the nineteenth and twentieth centuries, the tariff was used to protect home industry from foreign competition
unconstitutional — against the laws of the Constitution

INDEX